I Go With God

Written by Jill Ferrie
Illustrated by Muhammad Khaidir Syaféi
Designed by Nicolás Pacheco

FERRIETALES PUBLISHING, LLC
Cresco Iowa

I Go With God

Quote by Mary Baker Eddy used courtesy
of the Mary Baker Eddy Collection.

For information regarding permission
write to FerrieTales, 3690-318th Ave.,
Cresco, Iowa 52136

ISBN 978-0-9976560-0-8

Visit us at www.igowithgod.com

I Go With God
written by Jill Ferrie
illustrated by Muhammad Khaidir Syaféi
designed by Nicolás Pacheco

Dear reader,

I Go With God builds on the spiritual healing truth that "God is our refuge and strength, a very present help in trouble" (Psalms 46:1) as discovered by everyday people in our favorite Bible stories. In this story a young boy shows us that God's power is as present for us today as it was years ago. He also helps us understand that:

- God is Spirit and, therefore, He is ever-present.

- Prayer helps us feel God's presence and love.

- Angels are God's way of helping us.

Angels are defined as "God's thoughts passing to man;..." in the Christian Science textbook, *Science and Health with Key to the Scriptures* by Mary Baker Eddy (p. 581). As such, when we pray, we can all hear His healing thoughts in our time of need.

As the young boy in this story learns, "Listening to God is a good way to pray. His angels chase all those bad feelings away."

Puffer's my goldfish,
he swims in a bowl.
I feed him by nine,
at least that's my goal.

But something was wrong,
I felt really bad.
I wasn't myself,
I got very sad.

My tummy felt sick.
My head was too hot.
This was not good.
Oh no, it was not!

I needed help fast,
I had a big day.
My friend's birthday party
was hours away.

I sat down to think
on the edge of my bed.
I usually make it
when Puffer is fed.

But I wasn't up
for doing that job.

I wanted to lie on that bed
like a blob.

Then I remembered
the best help that I knew,
our Father in heaven,
God -- you know Him too.

God is Spirit,
He fills every spot.
In fact, there's no place
where His power is not.

So I prayed to God
like I know how to do.
When I pray I get quiet.
What
do
you
do?

I closed my eyes
and rested my head
to listen to God,
to hear what He said.

Good thoughts filled my mind—
they floated right in.

Good thoughts are angels.
I started to grin.

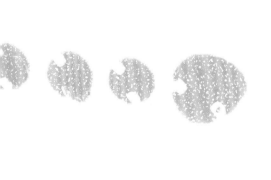

God gives us those angels,
they're easy to hear-

right when we need them,
they're helpful and clear...

like paying attention
when crossing the street
so cars passing by
don't run over our feet.

Angels kept coming
and filling my mind.

My thoughts were all happy
and loving and kind...

like hugging a friend
to show her I care,

and laughing so hard
that I fall off my chair,

and singing and dancing
and helping my neighbor

Rusty!

find her lost cat
named Rusty Van Sleighbor.

I suddenly noticed
I felt so much better.
I jumped up from my bed
and put on my red sweater.

Like the air that I breathe but don't ever see, the **power of prayer** is always with me.

Listening to God is a good way to pray.
His angels chase all those bad feelings away.

So when you need help,
just ask God, it's all cool.
He's everywhere you are,
even at school.

Wherever you go,
whatever you do,
His angels go with you.
They go with me too.

I made my bed quickly
and picked up my toys.

I ran to my Puffer,
he made a strange noise.

patience

Puffer was gasping
for air- it was bad.
He swam on his side
and he looked very sad.

Blurp

Blurp

Blurp

Well I did the best thing
that a person could do,
I asked God for help.
You can pray that way too.

Puffer likes music
so I sang him a prayer.
Singing can help you
feel safe in God's care.

Angels

God is always with us,
His angels help us out.

They give us good ideas
like things to sing about.

Angels make us happy,
they help us feel good too.

We can trust His angels,
they're here for me and you.

Then I got really close
to my Puffer and said,

*"God made you all good
from your tail to your head."*

He felt it! He got it!
It was easy to see

that God helped my Puffer
just like He helped me.

And so it was time
to be on my way.
I left for the party,
ready to play.

Wherever I go,
whatever I do,
I go with God.
You go with Him too!

Can you get Puffer to his bowl?